BEHIND THE
MASK

AUTHOR
JAMMIE LOCKETT

Copyright © 2019 by Jammie Lockett.

All rights reserved. No part of this book may be reproduced in any form or by any electronic or mechanical means, including information storage and retrieval systems, without permission in writing from the publisher, except by reviewers, who may quote brief passages in a review.

This publication contains the opinions and ideas of its author. It is intended to provide helpful and informative material on the subjects addressed in the publication. The author and publisher specifically disclaim all responsibility for any liability, loss, or risk, personal or otherwise, which is incurred as a consequence, directly or indirectly, of the use and application of any of the contents of this book.

WRITERS REPUBLIC L.L.C.
515 Summit Ave. Unit R1
Union City, NJ 07087, USA

Website: *www.writersrepublic.com*
Hotline: *1-877-656-6838*
Email: *info@writersrepublic.com*

Ordering Information:
Quantity sales. Special discounts are available on quantity purchases by corporations, associations, and others. For details, contact the publisher at the address above.

Library of Congress Control Number: 2019950682
ISBN-13:   978-1-64620-072-6   [Paperback Edition]
               978-1-64620-073-3   [Digital Edition]

Rev. date: 09/16/2019

I want to thank God and my strong mother for giving me a chance to leave a mark on this world. I would also like to thank my sisters and brothers for believing in me throughout this journey and the rest of my loved ones as well. Loyalty gets tested as you grow with life and the different obstacles along the way so I want to show my gratitude for the ones who have held me up and loved me unconditionally no matter what life has thrown.

DEAR MAMA

All the sacrifices and cold nights
I seen you cry and just wanted to hold you tight

Everyday you broke your back to put food on the plate, to make sure we all ate

Many obstacles, you was grown so young
You never turned your back on us even when we bounced from home to home

I love you unconditionally from my heart to my soul
You my best friend, you got a heart full of gold

Your strength is admirable, I owe you the world
Faced with poverty and unfortunate circumstances

As a single mother you still took chances
Raised four bad kids on your own
You gave me a chance to write my own song

Beautiful black Queen I'm proud of you
You installed morals and principles in me
I'll always hold you to the highest degree

Before your last breath, I hope to retire you
Buy you a big house and watch you smile

Thank you for teaching me how to hold it down

I love you

STAY TRUE

Every man is defined by his reaction to any given situation
I know you had it hard but why you waiting
Being complacent is a choice
From the time you was born, your story started
Grew up in pain, I understand why you cold-hearted
Forty years later, you still jaded
No legacy on the table, now your last name out-dated
Now you living vicariously through your kids, telling stories about what you could've did
Society don't give a fuck if you down on your luck
Get up and hustle or continue to be stuck
Dreams turn into nightmares real fast
Get your grind up or come in last
Don't be that old dude always reminiscing about the past

AMBITION

I'm conflicted but gifted
Blessed with elite precision
Carry me with 6 if I'm ever mediocre
Perseverance is a work of art
It doesn't matter where you start
Get it out the mud and play your part
Society will test your heart
How much do you value your integrity
Have you ever dreamed about being wealthy
Thirst for validation blinds the eye to what success means
False perception may be your demise if you fall for anything under the skies
A wise man knows he knows nothing
I continue to educate myself and stay in my own lane
Don't get tricked out of your position by playing these games
Immaculate catastrophe is destined for the one who follows and it saddens me
Be a student of life and love thyself
Strive for unity and wealth
May your impact be felt
Find a purpose you're willing to die for
Manifest with confidence
Cut ties with this cycle of pain
At the end of the day you have too much to gain

DIVINE PRESENCE

Damn lotus how you shake free
When the stars align you where you supposed to be
Divine presence I seen you in a dream
You the realist of them all, I just wish I could call
Baby you one of one, just being blunt
Although complexity lies in your eyes
I can't say I'm surprised
Such aura with a scent of heaven
What a divine presence
Attempted to approach you to finding half stepping and ended up in second
Not to be selfish but I want you all to myself and, can I cherish your complexion
Message in the bottle can you come teach me a lesson
Stop second guessing and let me be the reason you stop stressing
Can I love you under the sun
After every moon, I swear you the only one
I've had enough fun, please don't run
Ignore the perception and misconception
I understand the pain you endured as a adolescent
May the universe heal you for all you have been threw
I thanked God soon as he sent you

PRODUCT OF MY ENVIRONMENT

No reasoning for the broken one
Scars cut so deep hindered him from being the chosen one
Loaded gun but I won't run
Shake back and let's have fun
Momma crying, bullets flying
Product of my community, I swear I'm not lying
Back against the wall
Threw the pain, I must stand tall
Pressure in my face, I just wanted to ball
Surrounded by toxic masculinity, 40 shells and Hennessy
I thought you was a friend of me
Envy in your eyes, you slowly became my enemy
Victim of the streets
Systematically oppressed, it's hard to see that I was blessed
Let's be realistic, I was born to be a statistic
I forgot to mention
From here it's only death or prison

WAKE UP

Poverty allows the indignity of the rich to feed off the flesh of the weak
400 years of slavery and they still want me to be humble and weak

I am the black sheep of the land of the free
Home of the brave but we scared to sleep
Claims of diversity but they gentrified the streets

You say I'm a minority so subconsciously I'll never be free
Truth is you really scared of me

The unapologetic black man with a book in his hand
Knife at my throat the and still I stand

No hand out, even if I have to stand alone
I'll never sell out
Systematically we are often defined by who you'd rather us be

We are not objects, we are the catalyst to progress
As we disgust the injustice and dissect the mass incineration brought to you by the leader of our nation

You want to build a wall and eliminate immigration but letting killer cops receive paid vacations

LAND OF THE INJUSTICE

I thought the land of the free had open arms
You separating families forcefully so how can you stand to see your reflection
How can you put a kid in a cage and say behave

Morally it's sad to see
Example of why we have to unite and bridge the disconnect and gain better intellect

We have to get rid of liabilities and fill the vacancies
More activist and less make believes
Sincere motives and more legacies
We have to love one another in order to be set free

Until then the cycle will never end
My brother and sister with you I stand

LACK OF COMMUNICATION

Misconceptions of me not fucking with you
I hit you up and told you to fall threw
You didn't respond
Let's rewind
Was it my fault or did I hit you at a bad time

I told you I wanted you but you needed proof
Toxic masculinity didn't allow me to see it threw
This time around you didn't answer cause you had a new boo

I guess this what happens when you wait too long
Feelings so strong but you felt like you waited up and stayed too long

Shame on me
At one point it was mutual with the energy you was giving me
Outside forces intervened and we was no longer a team

Now we stuck with would could have been
Guilty conscience weighing in now we not even friends

INTENTIONS

We have to stop the cycle of who will fall first
Should I hit you or wait on you
Modern day relationships are based off illusions these days
Which games are you willing to play
Which toxic situationship is more fun

I swear loving you is what I meant to do
Now intentions are blurred
If we don't stop this cycle "I hate you" will forever be our last words

3 A.M

Your heart is fragile, I understand that
Let me know how to treat you, I know you demand that

I'm willing to understand the pain in your eyes and get use to the light in your soul
You come from a broken past, I know how that goes

I'm not trying to replace
My intentions are to restore, the beautiful art that was damaged behind closed doors
My past is my past, yours is yours

Can I be your motivation on your rise to your aspirations
I'm willing to understand why your past complications led to your current situation

Can you communicate instead of overstate comparisons
When I visualize you I see gold, I pray that you don't fold
Continue to be bold cause I like that shit

I PROMISE

I want to be your friend and your Confidant
The root of the problem be where the truth lies
Instead of searching for truth we lie and hide

I'm not normal, sometimes I sit for hours straight, can I call you when it gets late
I respect you for being who holds us together

No I don't completely know you but I'm willing to
I'm willing to show you that the old you can grow too

I admire you
I promise to abide by the boundaries you allow me to
My focus is on you

The Apple in your eyes tell the truth
You was the truth from the start, but nobody cherished your heart
This is where it starts

I promise you'll be able to tell me apart
Bless

PEACE

Purified sanity and less vanity
To what degree is the sacrifice too high

Toxic energy can't stand next to me
Every time it gets the best of me

Negative insights and bad vibes
Constant complaints of this life of mine

I got time today
Let's unwind today
Let peace lead you to love and let's find our way

Yesterday was tough but that was yesterday
Hope that brighter days will knock the pain away
Still I mediate and pray

We can't stray away from healthy relationship in exchange for toxic fun
Everything is beautiful under the sun

EVERYTHING IS EVERYTHING

Times get difficult and we run to temporary satisfaction
We fool everyone with a decent caption

People fall in love with the illusion instead of what's really going on
Hard times defines your character
Will you fold or will you get bold and take chances

Protect your sanity at all cost
The energy we possess is not bought
Find peace by unlearning what you were taught

Control your narrative and stay present
This peace is heaven sent
I pray that your spirits remain so precious and elegant
I hold you to higher standards and you'll always be relevant

Organic arrangements and sincere motives
Love is peace
Peace is love
Remain solid and pursue all of the above

LOVE IS,

Often we fall in love with the idea of love because that's the only hope for us
I still ask what is love

Ever seen the reflection of your soul and been satisfied
Love is not defined by how those feel of you
It's the purified energy within you and the aura you possess

We often obsess with validation and meaningless conversations

Manifest self preservation and appreciation through rapid maturation
The constant void we try to feel with someone else is an illusion until we love ourselves

Often we compromise true self when around peers because we don't know true self when we are alone

Your purified energy is meant to attract those who are right for you

TOXICITY

The best drugs are bad for you
That's why toxic energy is so compatible
What would you rather do
Continue to settle for less and be miserable
Or love thyself, be loved and treated magical

The preference is obvious but we continue to be irrational
This takes me back to the root of the problem

Do you know thyself, or are you highly dependent on validation from someone else

Love doesn't have to be an illusion if we can stop the confusion
All this toxic masculinity, pride, and generational, emotional and physical abusing

Love is peace
Love is grace
Love is the universe
Love is you

What is life if love is not the glue
I love me and I love you

THE CYCLE CONTINUES

How many times is the last time
Soft cries and passive vibes
You so elusive these days
So exclusive you should of stayed
I treated you regular and you ran away
This what happens when we wait to long
The one that got away is my theme song
Feelings so strong but it wasn't mutual
I got use to you and got too comfortable
Too often I forgot to cherish why I fell in love with you
I took you for granted and it took you leaving for me to understand it
I say ima change like every time
Same bullshit, same line
Idea was fun but it wasn't our time
They say if I really love you I should let you go
If this is the truth, I want to let you know
The art inside of you is beautiful
It was a pleasure to share your energy
When your soul flourish I hope you remember me

POVERTY NORMS

Moral philosophy but to what degree

Not a ounce of care for the life you just took
Based on the street conception, you just going by the book

You kill mine, I kill yours
The mind of an assassin will cause havoc in a dramatic fashion

Rats getting bold, lies getting told
Crazy how this street code unfold

The game being sold to the highest bidder
Cut my sentence and I'll find the killer

Meanwhile, My mom is crying laying her son to rest
This is a cycle of destruction, whose going to clean up the mess

I can't get this pain off my chest so I'll shoot until there's nothing less
Traumatized and my mom is stressed
This the game I know best

STATISTIC

According to social media I'm a menace
When I was born they already gave me a prison sentence
With a rap sheet a mile long
I know this a sad song but this is what's going on
Our kids scared to walk home

What if I don't want to rap or play ball
Can I still call
Will you still believe in me at all
Why do I have to hide my flaws

Mesmerized by these lies
I'm sick of trying to just survive

I want to build a legacy
Show America a better me
Build society from the ground up
Show people that this is not us

Trials and tribulations is what shapes you
Hard work and dedication is what makes you

Eliminate the excuses and aim high
Love more and get rid of that pride
Stay focused no matter the time
Protect your brother and sister and let's rise

I see greatness in your eyes

REASSURANCE

I know you say you love me from a distance
I just wanted to hear it again

I pick up my pen, not to sound desperate
but to see you again
I hope you understand
The pain that lies within makes me feel less than man

I wanted to please you while pleasing myself too
A love like you is one in a million
The makeup after a breakup, what a wonderful feeling
Our downfall was sexual healing, what a lustful shame

I understand you doing you and I'm doing me, whose to blame
Hope that one day we can still intervene
Unwind the simple things

Keep your jeans on, I want to understand how you still so head strong
Why did we wait to communicate for so long

A simple conversation of when did ya hair get so long?
You not one for small talk
I just wanted to hear your voice
At one point I really wanted to marry you and it was really your choice

Unpopular belief made it impossible for me
You settled for less of course
At this rate you gearing up for a divorce

No intentions of extorting your heart
I'm not perfect but I knew from the start
Perception vs Reality would ruin us and tear us apart

Bless your heart stay true, so I can always love you for you

PUBLIC ENEMY

The complexion of my skin makes me sin
According to the man

Walk in my shoes and try to understand
Equality in America is quick sand
Present in the moment and never spoken of again

Gun loaded at my head
I can't breath or I'm dead

If my mama cry, you get a vacation
Your hate for me is motivation
You can't stand toe to toe with me like segregation

The opposition conditions us as if this still a plantation
Fights for unity but y'all causing separation

Look at the border, man that shit causing frustration
Toddlers facing starvation
Land of the free but yet we feen for salvation
Thanks to the leader of our nation

In need of meditation, Ease my mind
It's time to apply pressure, and end this mediocre life cycle and senseless crime

Stay woke and stay present when it's time to represent

The strength we possess is heaven sent not controlled by a president

Fight for your brother and sister at all times not just when we feel it's relevant

KING NIP

King Nip paved the way
Gave young hustlas hope for a better day
In his name I pray

Still in his name we stray
No need for passive activist on this rainy day

Metaphorically elite
It's in my heart to preach and hope to reach
The masses affected by violence in these streets

Nip showed us a way to eat
On our own plate
The envious appetite never ate so he prey
Once again in his name I pray
If you want a hand out we could never relate

He was teaching us how to code
Jealousy and envy intervened and his killer got bold
God bless his soul

May his spirits live on
He built a computer out of his own home
Taught us gentrification didn't have to stop wealth
If we band together we can protect ourselves

Showed us how to build a legacy with equity and it stuck with me
Even though his efforts was cut short unfortunately, I see

The message in the bottle under the tree
We have to be willing to search under the debris and escape oppression so our souls could be free

I see you and you see me
If I kill you, I kill me
You're the mere reflection of we

Let's continue the marathon, not this cycle
I pray Nip, one day I could have a impact just like you

#LongLiveTheGreat

A GODDESS

I appreciate you for being modest
You know you the shit if we being honest

From the look in your eyes I can tell you've been emotionally abused
but your strength and perseverance is timeless
Outside looking in, I can tell you got it

Focused young Queen, I seen you in a dream
Maybe an illusion or maybe it is what it seems
May the universe bring you sanity
May your energy be purified
and your soul stress free

You're merely the reflection of a muse
You gave these niggas clues and they still tried to play you

I appreciate whoever raised you
Beloved, continue to be true to self

Don't allow anyone to devalue you
May your strength continue to carry you threw and all your dreams come true

I ADORE YOU

I sense your vibe, it's heaven sent
Purified skin, so immaculate
Beautiful mind, relevant
If I was blind, your aura could represent

Sparks fly out of the corner of your eyes
Your unique presence can't be denied
If I'm not the one
I want to know I tried
Powerful woman, who the weak minded may despise

A true work of art, where do I start
Provide me with clarity and I'll play my part

She said provide me with sanity and allow me to be free of vanity
The man that stands next to me has to be the one who appreciates me
I'll love you with everything within me if your not afraid to blend with me

Do you admire me for me or for who I am with you
Since you love transparency, can you see all the pain I've been threw

I can't give you all of me because that's too precious
But I can appreciate you for the blessing, that you are

I don't mean to act tough nor hard, but I came to far
I was alone but I found myself now look where we are

You approached me regularly
I'm a Queen, you lucky to stand next to me
Don't be shook, just come correct
Forget a perception, let's keep this in context

Respect me or I have to respectively say thank you, next

MY CONFIDANT

She said she loved me but it was seasonal
I hated you after I integrated you
Into my lifestyle
Situation was wild
Love at first sight, you could've had my child
Lost in the sauce, your ingredients made me smile

For a while it was a sad song
Wondering if it wasn't you then who
You was my confidant
My go to in the morning time
Until summertime

I prayed that this was the one
Like Last time
Now I frown in disbelief
Filled with unpleasantries
Beautiful sight when you came
I hated when you was ready to leave

Soul ties lie deep
Soil thickens under the tree
You could've used me but you abused me emotionally

Thought you was heaven sent
The smell of your delicate scent made me convinced
Astonishing complexion made me submit
Toxic masculinity made it hard to commit
You seen threw me no tent

I came for you when you didn't send
I fed you lies and then I ran
Then pondered on why it happened to me again

Self-reflection kicked in
In realization that my lust for you was sin

Every time I devalue my Queen
I fail the next generation of men
Now I'm my father all over again
When does the cycle end

QUEEN, I STAN

She pleaded for me to be gentle
I asked why

She responded and said I've been broken before
Open dialogue while our clothes on the floor

As I looked into your eyes
It was clear the pain you endured

Your strength made it easy to ignore
I'm sorry that my concern for you was poor

Mindset on one thing when you hit the door
While you screamed for help
The world ignored

The perception of being bitter
Yea, I know you've heard it before
Feeling powerless as they only judge you by your contour

Your perfect imperfection is admirable

Why do we wait till you lash out to acknowledge you
Fed you to the zoo instead of protecting you
Too many thoughts of undressing you

World full of flawed humans but you get the blame
Now I understand the thirst for validation because you no longer feel the same

Unappreciated, now your love is outdated
Now I understand the pressures you must withstand
My admiration for you has grown, now I Stan

The pleasantries of your heart and soul made me a man
Protecting you at all cost should be priority even though last time I ran

Queen, let your integrity and perseverance set you free

You have been the realist of us all
I'm saddened that I was too blind to see

SET US FREE

I feed you jewels with grace
Say amen

Being marginalized and traumatized by the man

How can one not sin
How much toxic energy can one with stand

400 years apparently
or Apparently we are released in the minds of the bland and
land of the free
How can you not see?

Subconsciously trapped in a muse
Don't be confused

Illusions turnt reality
It's really sad to see
Do you feel powerless like a casualty?
Then why you approaching so casually?
Usually I feel bad but you see....
Your not a casualty
And it saddens me

Fuck a perception
You are your reality

The unknown is irrelevant
Embrace it because it's heaven sent

Stay dangerous
Stop being so complacent

Seek Peace not praise
Don't let love fade away
Stay present even through rainy days
Bless

ENOUGH IS ENOUGH

The pressure, trials and tribulations of the everyday life
Who am I not to sacrifice

When expectations exceed what they were
betting against do we celebrate?
What is a victory if we still not free?
A win is not a win if it comes from blatant sin upon the peers you represent

Truth be told....they told us lies...now how do we unlearn all the bullshit they televise.
Don't get me wrong I love a bad bit** with skimpy clothes
Although the physical representation doesn't allow her heart to show
Soulful Queen, I hope you know, without you the very seeds of this universe would explode

It's time to unlearn the incompetence of a white society that we have recently exposed
We are hated because we are powerful not because we are less

The very foundation we walk upon was blessed by the best......Goddess and King
You know the rest
Stay blessed

Let's control the narrative and embrace the rest
Don't stress, be great
Now we can embark confidently on this journey now that we know what's at stake

HE WAS UNARMED

The shade of his skin made him a threat
He couldn't afford food but all of a sudden
He could afford a tech
He reached for his wallet
They aimed for his neck
Home from college
Vacation to the morgue
His mother crying
Asking why my son and not yours
Another closed door
Another lost soul
Welcome to Amerikkka
You know how this story goes
Gentrified neighborhoods
Racist CEO's
The life of a black man is undervalued
Kill us today and next week they over shadow you
Stay dangerous black men
They hate to see us win

THE FALL

Pain lies deep
What a treat, as I sob sarcastically
All these years I thought everything toxic
Was for me
I'm paralyzed emotionally
Always missed that physical touch
Because love was too much
I can't Phaethon the rain without you
Cuts so deep I couldn't heal without you
Humbled soul weakened by disloyalty
Toxicity, masculinity
Illusions created false reality
Nothing's real to me
As I wiggle threw this phase
This pain will shape me
To face you one day
I Pray

THE RISE

Elevation and mindfulness
I seek truth if it exist
As I cling to books looking for the right script
Painting an illusion as life continues to midst
If we don't take a risk
Hope for the next generation doesn't exist
Subconsciously we are sick
Daily norms and trendy clicks
How can we heal if not a soul commits
I cry in hopes that our time comes
I'll smile in joy and peace when we appreciate all as one
Can we love under one sun

A REAL ONE

You a real one
Baby let's go have some real fun
You opened up so deep
I kissed you on your cheek
Your aura smells so sweet

Smile on your face
All that pain was a disgrace
You a one of one
Not a soul can take your place

Can you stay up late
Can you fix me a plate
Tell me about your day
You a real one that's why we relate

I appreciate you
You respect my grind
Every time we link
It's a wonderful time
Say Queen

Can you forever be mine

WITHOUT LOVE

Without love we are merely the reflection of what we hate

The aura you possess is the outcome of self-reflection not neglection of true self or validation

So much hate in our nation
Love the neighbor with appreciation

It's devastating that the leader of our nation is a blatant racist Caucasian

How could Amerikkka choose this bigot for representation
We are in the state of depression and separation

Anxiety and the oppression inside of me is not what defines me
If we can unite and love one another we can change the mere perception of humankind
Our faith will be restored, and the sun will still shine
Or we can remain blind and act like we not losing time

Empower those around you and stay true to self
Don't be afraid to ask for help

Life is not guaranteed so who would you rather be?
The person who gives up or the one who fights to be set free
As long as you are blessed with breath it's your decision
Without love we are imbeciles
That's why times like these are so critical
The correlation is that we are the foundation
So, let's go get back our nation

FREE GAME

We can't gain ownership by playing it safe
Often, we allow the fear of defeat to control our subconscious

I'm building sweat equity to produce a better me
Organically our anatomy is a form of artistry
Through history our inner cities are clustered with misery

Hoop dreams or pick up a mic even if your rhymes not tight
We are conditioned to work a 9-5 even if they not treating us right

By forty we praying for a 401k and better days
At fifty we reminiscing about how our dreams slipped away
Surrounded by self-hate, hoping that this pain goes away

Society sets us up for a catastrophe
Still I strive for lavish days in hopes that God shows me a way
Set up a blueprint and don't stray away

The struggle is inevitable but what would you rather do
Die working a 9-5 or give your kids something to look forward too

Build a legacy and keep your integrity
Go against the grain when this world tries to drive you insane

Only a fool doesn't change
You can either break the cycle or remain the same

SUMMER NIGHTS

Devil in a tight dress
I know you prayed for times like this
As I caress your thighs and rise to your breast
I'll take my time out of respect
Beautiful complexion, can't believe I was second guessing
Let me ease your mind, I know you been stressing
Stuck on this grind
I haven't made time to appreciate this blessing
Your presence was heaven sent
I prayed for a vibe like this
Maybe one day we can reminisce on how such work of art exist
You are one of one, this is more than just having fun

THE ART OF HUSTLE

Beauty in the eye of struggle
Will I fold or will I hustle
You must love the game
When you down on your luck it will drive you insane
Where your heart at
Are you caught up in perception or reality?
Would you rather be rich or wealthy with a legacy?
Would you rather look like you have it or really be about it?
See, integrity is the purest form of your heart
When your back against the wall, can you play your part?
The divine spirits within your soul keeps you whole
You possess the power, but will you fold?
Study the game because it's never sold
A wise man never told
He observed the game inch by inch and load by load
Then he watched his blueprint unfold
The art of hustle remains

MANIFESTATION

When the earth shifts and the stars don't align, don't stop the grind

The universe is where it's suppose to be
Whatever burden you are carrying is temporary

Ignore the perception about where you ought to be
In reality your time is coming and blessings will flow in abundance

Keep your sanity, don't lose yourself to vanity and earthly things
Strengthen your spirit and flourish into the atmosphere

Love thy neighbor with all you got
Stay focused on your dreams and aspirations
Match manifestation with preparation

Clean up toxic waste and get rid of self-hate
Rather you early or late, continue to prepare your plate
Have faith that God will keep you safe and remove the fake

Be all you can be and don't stop until your soul is set free
Set the world on fire and keep going higher and higher

THE TRUTH

I thought everything was mutual
You said this what you wanted then acted unusual

I should've fed you casual conversation and dope dick
Instead I took a risk and gave you all of me

I tried to be different than the last time
Should've tapped into my intuition and made a wiser decision

Your potential was enticing, so I didn't pay attention and you caught me slipping

Claims of being so real but you folded

I gave you transparency and you gave me this
Now eat this subliminal till you cease to exist

Money ain't shit just don't waste my time
Y'all lie like telling the truth is a crime
This is why being a dog is a preferred good time

The misconception that the man is the one who does the neglecting, but in reality the real ones face the most rejection

I would've never put you second
You taught me a valuable lesson
When the stars don't align, just accept it and let it rhyme

My pride let you stay by my side
I offered you a better me, now I'm cold-hearted cooking up a recipe

Your not a real one, that's an illusion
Super average, I hope there's no confusion

I gave you the best of me, now here's the conclusion

Milton Keynes UK
Ingram Content Group UK Ltd.
UKHW030019180324
439604UK00001B/243